0177230

£10.95.

WILLIAM TALMAN

Maverick Architect

STUDIES IN ARCHITECTURE

Series editors: JOHN HARRIS and MARCUS BINNEY

WILLIAM TALMAN

Maverick Architect

JOHN HARRIS

London
GEORGE ALLEN AND UNWIN
Boston   Sydney

George Allen & Unwin (Publishers) Ltd,
40 Museum Street, London WC1A 1LU, UK

George Allen & Unwin (Publishers) Ltd,
Park Lane, Hemel Hempstead, Herts HP2 4TE, UK

Allen & Unwin Inc.,
9 Winchester Terrace, Winchester, Mass 01890, USA

George Allen & Unwin Australia Pty Ltd,
8 Napier Street, North Sydney, NSW 2060, Australia

First published in 1982

British Library Cataloguing in Publication Data

Harris, John
  William Talman.
1. Talman, William   2. Architects – Great Britain – Biography
I. Title
720'.092'4   NA997.T/
ISBN 0-04-720024-3
ISBN 0-04-720025-1 Pbk

Set in 11 on 13 point Sabon by Computape (Pickering) Ltd,
and printed in Great Britain
by William Clowes Ltd, Beccles and London

for
HUGH and JOHN

Contents

List of illustrations

11

Preface

Exactly twenty-five years ago I began to inquire about William Talman. Howard Colvin's *Biographical Dictionary of British Architects* had just been published, and it seemed to me then, as it does now, that the leading country house architect of the Court of William III deserved a book. Alas, year succeeded year, and the task was like trying to run up a down escalator. However hard and relentless the search, nothing new appeared of any consequence. The evidence is in the comparison between Mr Colvin's 1954 entry and his 1978 one, the later is only a little richer than the earlier, and there still remain tantalising attributions: Hackwood, Blyth, Waldershare, Panton, Bretby, Wanstead. Happily Merlin Unwin has had the courage to launch this new biographical series, and I have been persuaded to pull together my notes and produce a small book. It is not, I believe, a proper memorial, for Talman deserves a monograph on the scale of those dedicated to Vanbrugh and Hawksmoor. They, and especially James Gibbs, inherited much from him, and even with the evidence as it stands he meddled in more country houses than all his chief contemporaries put together. I am conscious that my division of material is not satisfactory, but how do you categorise an architect who was so omnivorous and whose spectrum of styles was so wide? For this reason I have divided up his practice into a number of categories: the years of establishment; the obvious concurrent works at Chatsworth and Burghley; what I call his maverick style epitomised by Drayton, or his excursion into a Spartan brick style as at Kimberley. If it breaks up his career into a number of compartments, he is, nevertheless, better understood. He has always fascinated me and I hope I have done my duty to him in the compass of this petite monograph.

Acknowledgments

Having ruminated upon Talman for a quarter of a century I am indebted to many friends for the fertility of conversation. I cannot list everyone but from memory I must especially remember Dr Kerry Downes, our historian of baroque architecture who could have written this little book better than I, Mr Marcus Binney, Mr Timothy Connor, Mr John Cornforth, and Dr Terry Friedman, and my old travelling friend Derek Sherborn. There is a special thanks to Mr Howard Colvin with whom we all share our discoveries.

Photographic acknowledgments

All Souls College, Oxford 13; Ashmolean Museum, Oxford 17; British Architectural Library 5, 8, 11, 14, 18, 40–1, 43–5, 51–7, 59, 62–5, 72, 82; British Library 74; British Museum 20–1; Christies 4; Country Life 6, 25–9, 39, 87; Courtauld Institute of Art 15–16; A. F. Kersting 35, 88; Jeremy Lever 77; National Monuments Record 12, 22, 24, 30, 32–3, 38, 76, 78; John Newman 81; Rijksdienst v/d Monumentenzorg 7; Sir John Soane's Museum 59–61, 66–70; United Grand Lodge of England 1; Victoria and Albert Museum 36–7, 42, 46, 48–50, 58; Wightscot Ltd 75; Witt Collection 2–3.

1 A beginning and an end

The career of William Talman (Plate 1) reached a zenith in 1702 when, following the death of William III, his patent for the Comptrollership of the Works was not renewed. By that time he had built or altered at least a dozen country houses and was by repute the leading country house architect of the old Williamite Court. Nevertheless, despite all this he remains intangible both as an architect and a person; hardly any correspondence by or to him survives. His background was Wiltshire squirarchy of some affluence, and his father William lived at Eastcott Manor House near West Lavington. He was only fifteen when his father died in 1663 leaving the manor house and estate to an elder son Christopher, and to him the leasehold on three houses in King Street, Westminster. Apart from some genealogical facts, his early life and upbringing is a mystery. Indeed, the very first post-natal reference to him occurs as late as 1678 when he obtained the perk of King's Waiter in the Port of London, sharing this customs post with Thomas Apprice. Now Apprice belonged to the 2nd Earl of Clarendon's household, and as Talman is known to have lent Clarendon at least £800 before 1685,[1] and was to design his country seat at Swallowfield in Berkshire in 1689, evidently this lord was an early patron. Because Talman's first fully authenticated task was the rebuilding of Chatsworth from 1686, a task unlikely to have been given to a newcomer to architecture, it is inconceivable that his reputation had not already been supported by a respectable body of work. Chatsworth was certainly not the only credential for him to be appointed Comptroller of the Royal Works in May 1689, second in command only to Wren. Two attributed houses bear his imprimatur, both were started in 1683: Hackwood Park, Hampshire, for the 6th Marquess of Winchester and Blyth Hall,

17

Nottinghamshire, for Edward Mellish. They advance in their respective ways the typology of the country house. If these are Talman's first independent works as a professional, his training, even if acquired in a gentlemanly capacity, must have taken place during the preceding ten years. During this period, among the architects practising then, such as Wren, Hooke, Samwell, Winde or May, it is May alone whose works can be regarded as a reservoir for Talman's developing style from 1683.

It is therefore worthwhile to examine May's achievement after 1660 when he had returned from exile. Eltham Lodge, Kent, of 1664 is Dutch inspired, but inside May had already begun to display his interest in spatially complex stairs, thus departing from the usual Jonesian static plan. At Eltham there is a visual link between the two stairs across an intervening passage. A year later he was the architect for Berkeley House in Piccadilly, prominently placed and therefore as influential as Clarendon House, its neighbour. Here was a brick, stone-coigned, hipped-roof house with quadrant colonnades tied to offices flanking a forecourt, and thus prophetic of Hackwood. Unfortunately no plan of Berkeley House survives, which is a pity. From 1669 May was Talman's predecessor as Comptroller of the Works, and in this capacity, and as Comptroller of the Works at Windsor from 1674, he began the remodelling of the Upper Ward there from 1675. Even if Talman was not involved officially at Windsor, he must have studied it well, for there and at Cassiobury Park, Hertfordshire, begun by May in 1676 for the Earl of Essex, is contained a vocabulary of planning and decoration germaine to Talman's future style. It recognises the wall as a potentially plastic enclosure made illusionistic by a combination of mural painting, sculptural plasterwork and carved woodwork, the work of, respectively, Antonio Verrio, John Grove and Grinling Gibbons who was assisted by Henry Phillips, Master Sculptor and Carver in Wood to the Works. The plan contributed to the spatial effect with vestibules and ingenious stairs of innovative and baroque design. At Cassiobury occurred the first oval in English domestic planning, and in its proper baroque way it was painted by Verrio and opened into a T-shaped loggia with a three-bay arcade. Another Dutch and baroque introduction was sculptured tympanums to the pediment of the entrance pilaster portico and to that on the astylar flanks. Cassiobury's interiors were a simplified version of Windsor's more regal ones, but here once again possibly Grove and certainly Gibbons were at work. Windsor and Cassiobury lead directly to Chatsworth and Burghley.

May's success and authority was partly due to his intelligent study of continental buildings, particularly in Holland and France where he is known to have travelled from 1656 to 1660. Talman is quite a different matter, for there is no evidence of foreign travel which meant that he acquired his idiosyncratic and maverick style from books and prints in addition to a first-hand examination of the latest fashions in English architecture. In this it is necessary to judge Talman as a collector and connoisseur. In 1713 he stated that he had made, 'and is still collecting by his son abroad, the most valuable Collection of Books, Prints, Drawings &c, as is in any one person's hands in Europe, as all the artists in Towne well know.'[2] This was no mean boast, for the Talman collection marked by his monogram of three interlaced Ts was celebrated and may well have been the largest private collection of architectural resources in the world.[3] From inventories and sale catalogues it is possible to reassemble a distinguished collection of pictures, bronzes and marbles.[4] By the late 1690s William had acquired the bulk of the designs by Palladio, Jones and Webb which today comprise the Burlington-Devonshire Collection at the Royal Institute of British Architects and at Chatsworth. All this could be regarded as a limitless quarry from which Talman could obtain ideas for both planning and the cosmetic of exteriors. Clearly he strove to be different, and all his works bear some quirk that is Talmanic, immediately identifiable, such as the many Trianon, Welbeck, or Haughton designs.

His acquisition of the Comptrollership in May 1689 may have been supported by Hans Bentinck,[5] created Earl of Portland in April and in June appointed Superintendent of the Royal Gardens with George London as Deputy Superintendent and Talman his Comptroller. This is the first official connection between the chief country house architect of the Williamite Court and the chief gardener who was to lay out nearly all Talman's gardens. The partnership is so consistent that a London garden may be assumed if the house had been built by Talman.

Talman's professional behaviour as an officer was autocratic. He was by no means subservient, either in his official dealings or in his personal relations with his clients. He never practised servility, and this frequently led to the termination of his employment. Sir John Vanbrugh, in his denigrating letter[6] to the Duke of Newcastle in 1703, wrote of the 'vexation and disappointment' shared by the Duke of Devonshire, Lord Carlisle, Sir John Germaine, Lady Falkland, Lord Coningsby, Lord Portmore and Lord Kingston. However, there is no proof that any complaint was made about bad workmanship or malpractice on Talman's part. He was simply a man of colic and irritability, of an affluent station in life which made him feel that there was no reason to bow and scrape. He would certainly have ousted Wren from his office of Surveyor if he had had the chance, but the tables were turned on him when William III died in 1702 and he was dismissed from the Comptrollership. This was by no means the end of his career, and it enabled him to spend more time on his mania for collecting, and to this end send his son John on long and frequent continental travels to study and collect.[7] In addition to living in the houses in King Street he had rooms in Grays Inn, and about 1702 had purchased land at Ranworth in Norfolk. It may have been about this time that John made a design (Plates 2–3) for an ideal house at Ranworth which reiterates many of the elements from the Trianon designs and included a long gallery fitted out as a library. Then in 1718 he purchased another house at Felmingham in the same county, and when he died on 22 November 1719 he was buried in Felmingham church under a black marble slab marked with the three interlaced Ts. He may have had some hope that his son would carry on his practice – borne out by the very large number of John's extravagantly baroque designs (Plate 4), all of an astounding fertility of invention. Architect he was not to be, and when John married a Frances Cockayne of Hinxworth in Hertfordshire in 1718, he settled down to the life of a gentleman. He was the first Director of the Society of Antiquaries and 'the indefatigable conservator of all that can be called curious, both of the present and past age.'[8] A description[9] of the Talman Collection at Hinxworth mentioned drawings and prints in over two hundred elephant folio volumes. It was this treasure house of ideas that William Talman drew upon for his free-ranging invention, resulting in a series of houses or house alterations between 1683 and 1710 that could be described as prophetic for later developments in planning and decoration in almost every case. He influenced all his contemporaries, and, in ways large or small, his buildings affected Sir John Vanbrugh and Nicholas Hawksmoor, John James and especially James Gibbs, and even if indirectly through the sale of the Palladio and Jones drawings to Lord Burlington, all the participants in the neo-Palladian movement.

2 The establishment of the Talman style

Two houses in Hampshire, Hackwood Park and Abbotstone, both built for the 6th Marquess of Winchester, merit comment in any account of Talman's career before he was elevated to the Comptrollership of the Works. Hackwood is a known quantity reconstructable from documents, whereas Abbotstone is a tantalising enigma. It appears that both were built at about the same time *c.* 1683, and what appears surprising is that both were hunting lodges. All that can be gathered about Abbotstone is a vague picture[10] of a small square building with a view through the house and the possibility of a cupola. The mystery is deepened by the existence of a site plan[11] showing a typical neo-Palladian square villa with canted bays on each front, set in the centre of converging avenues, and an elevation[12] of a domed rotunda of baroque detail inscribed for Abbotstone and for the 'Duke of B.' – the Duke of Bolton, Lord Winchester's title in 1689. The rotunda may well be by Giuseppe Grisoni, one of John Talman's Roman cronies and the probable author of the so-called John Talman sketch-book in the Witt Collection.[13] In any case what is astonishing about the site plan is how precocious it is for any date before *c.* 1720. Nothing more is known about Abbotstone[14] as built except that James Gibbs is reputed to have begun a great house here for the 2nd Duke of Bolton before his death in 1721, concurrent with works at Hackwood.

How Talman came to be patronised by Lord Winchester is unknown. What can be reconstructed[15] about Hackwood evokes a house that makes significant advances in planning. It was brick, stone-coigned at the angles, the main block nine bays wide with a pediment to the middle three bays, and from the front angles quadrant colonnades extended out to offices flanking a forecourt (Plate 5). In all this Hackwood was clearly a reflection of Berkeley House in Piccadilly. However, it possessed certain idiosyncracies in that the main block was only one room wide and from its ends were lateral extensions in the form of two corridors to small pavilions or cabinets, each pair joined by either a portico *in antis* or a screen of columns. Astonishingly, the whole of this house today is cocooned in the rebuilding that was initiated by Samuel Wyatt in 1805 and completed by Lewis Wyatt. Hackwood is therefore an intermediate stage between the Jonesian Stoke Park, Northamptonshire, of *c.* 1630, Berkeley House, and the Château de Voorst in Holland. At Hackwood there survives much fine quality naturalistic carving in the manner of Grinling Gibbons, and a particularly luscious ceiling (Plate 6) that could be by Edward Goudge, of a similar style and quality to the ceiling above the staircase[16] at Blyth Hall, Nottinghamshire, also begun by Talman in 1683. As will be seen, Blyth likewise anticipates new directions in planning.

De Voorst in Holland was begun[17] in 1695 for Arnold Joost Van Keppel, William III's young, favourite courtier who in 1697 was created Earl of Albemarle. De Voorst was, in fact, a gift from the king, and the existence of a pear-wood model (Plate 7) of English construction is proof that it was commissioned in England and sent over for execution. In building it was changed by Jacques Le Romain who added many Netherlandish baroque details and altered the roof. Inside Daniel Marot decorated it in the baroque taste of the Hampton Court of William III upon which he had himself worked. The model is quintessentially English in every respect and could be by no other than an English architect, and of all candidates Talman would be the most favoured, not only by the king, but by that other Dutch courtier, Lord Portland, and by Marot with whom Talman seems to have maintained personal and professional links. The relationship with Berkeley House was made even before De Voorst was built, for Edward Southwell noted in his diary[18] that 'The Main Body will be like My Lrd Ranelagh's at Chelsey, to which will be added 2 wings: with Corridors or Galleries to Joyne them like Berkeley House.' De Voorst is compellingly prophetic of a type of country house popularised by Gibbs twenty years on: brick without coigns, 2–3–2 bays with two equally proportioned floors, and the centre pedimented. Gibbs's Kelmarsh of *c.* 1728 (Plate 8) is its heir, or the house for a gentleman in Yorkshire published as Plate 6 in his *Book of Architecture*, 1728. The plan of de Voorst is also Talmanic for the model contained the stairs set in the spine of the house each side of the hall, an arrangement that Talman consistently uses from the 1690s and may, indeed, have introduced to English planning.

De Voorst leads on to a consideration of Lord Normanby's vexations. Talman had incurred these by 1703, and they relate to the acquisition of old Arlington House, soon to be named Buckingham House after Normanby was elevated to a dukedom in March 1703. William Winde was certainly the builder of Buckingham House (Plates 9–10) from 1702, but Winde is not known to have been in the vanguard of fashion, and in *Vitruvius Britannicus* in 1715 Colen Campbell writes specifically that Winde only 'conducted' the building, implying that he was the builder not the designer. It may also not be a coincidence that immediately previous to Normanby's lease, Arlington House was rented by the Duke of Devonshire, for whom, of course, Talman had been working at Chatsworth and had made a design (Plate 11) before May 1694 for a conventional Pratt-like house 'designed to be built in Lambs Conduit Fields.' The possibility that Talman designed a replacement for Arlington House taken over by Normanby should not be dismissed. Here again is the restatement of the quadrant theme, and because of its central site the new Buckingham House was very fashionable indeed, its progeny spreading across England almost from the time of its building. It also introduced a new elevational formula, a nine bay front of two stories marked off by a cornice supporting an attic with a balustrade. Giant pilasters are at the angles and these and the pilaster portico are continued through the attic with pilaster strips terminated on the balustrade by statues on the skyline. In planning there were also Talmanic episodes; a low entrance hall, somewhat dark, opened into the stairs by an arcade, allowing the visitor to ascend up into a bright, light, painted space. This was the formula *c.* 1705 for Fetcham Park (Plate 75), where, as at Buckingham House, Talman was architect and Laguerre the mural painter. For the garden the London-Wise Brompton Nursery provided a layout.

The quadrant link could be regarded as a method of adding that extra spice of variety to the traditional relationship between the body of a house and its extremities. This quest for variety by Talman had manifested itself by his idiosyncratic use of lateral pavilions linked by columnar episodes, of the sort to appear in many of his Hampton Court Trianon designs and those for Welbeck or Haughton. In all his works he is apparently striving to be different, and this was as much evident at Blyth (Plate 12) as at Hackwood. Blyth is the first proper pavilion or tower house after Wilton, but for Talman the derivation is not necessarily Palladian as much Serlian, or Serlio via France, and on plan Talman was frequently experimenting with houses having pavilions at the angles. The first Montagu House in London, *c.* 1675, had such pavilions in the French manner, and these were capped by domes, but the pavilion was partly enclosed within the body of the plan, whereas at Blyth they project almost fully as occurs on many neo-Palladian houses, and proper too is the demarcation by cornices of the towers rising above the house from their parts below. Talman was preoccupied with the tower and pavilion idea throughout the late 1690s and is unquestionably the author[19] of an uninscribed sketch of a large country house (Plate 13) with lateral offices connected to the main body by straight colonnades. The plan is an epitome of Talman's method and could be by no other. Staircases are set in the spine each side of the hall and are linked across it by a gallery as in the unexecuted plan (Plate 14) for Kiveton Hall, Yorkshire. In this fascinating and prophetic design there is cross-breeding with William Samwell's Eaton Hall, Cheshire, 1675,[20] which also contains cabinets in the towers; or with Montagu House; and certainly with Sir Godfrey Kneller's house at Whitton in Middlesex, *c.* 1709,[21] and of uncertain authorship. Once again in this uninscribed country house sketch there are premonitions of Gibbs.[22]

The sketch is, however, no less tantalising than one of the Victoria and Albert Museum's sketch sheets which possess, in addition to the plan for Witham, Somerset, and two studies for the garden front of Dorchester House, Surrey, studies for two other houses (Plate 50), both unidentified. One is a plan and elevation of a French-styled design with single storey pavilions and offices arranged around a forecourt of 184 by 200 feet, this prefacing a narrower forecourt flanked by stables, and this in turn opening into the court of the house itself. Its elevation with arched windows and hipped roof terminated by cupolas, and arcades in the centre, seem related to the Dorchester House sketches, as indeed they must be in time, *c.* 1700. What is curious and unexpected with so large an assemblage of offices, is that the main body of the house is only one room wide, and rises surprisingly to appear above the roof line with a crenellated parapet. The other study is equally frustrating, for a large and massively handled front of six bays divided by attached giant banded columns and ending with a powerful horizontal cornice, as dramatic as Chatsworth's. That this is an idea for fronting an existing house is demonstrated by the unhappy placing of the doorway off centre in the fourth bay.

Any building without quirks deserves to be questioned if attributed to Talman. For this reason Uppark (Plate 15) and Stanstead (Plate 16) in Sussex, which are fairly standard renditions of a popular post-Restoration brick house of the Hooke type, ought to be eliminated even though the attribution rests with J. Dallaway in 1815.[23] Similarly the same criteria can be directed at Kiveton. Talman certainly made the first plan (Plate 14) which contains creditable Talmanic episodes such as the oval vestibule opening into an imperial stair and spine stairs linked across the hall by a gallery. Kiveton as built from March 1698 for the Duke of Leeds is quite different (Plate 17) with motifs such as the keyed *oeil de boeufs* foreign to Talman's vocabulary. In any case the house bears no relationship to the plan which is exactly the same date as one (Plate 18) for a small house inscribed to Mr Bond,[24] in which once again Talman has inserted an oval vestibule. Talman's diversion from the current hipped-roof style is best demonstrated by Swallowfield in Berkshire, built for Lord Clarendon from 1689.[25] The standard 2–7–2 elevation (Plate 20) has received a most astonishing and ornate doorway (Plate 19), not a little reminiscent of Tibaldi's doors in the west front of the Milan Duomo. Then round the corner are more surprises, for the front (Plate 21) was brought forward twice with broken pediments spanning the seven outer and three inner bays. Today Swallowfield is encased in William Atkinson's cement of 1820, but inside there is an oval vestibule and remains of rich Goudge-style plasterwork. The quirks in Swallowfield, the idiosyncracies of planning in Hackwood or Blyth, all lead up to the culmination of Talman's maverick style from the Trianon projects to Drayton.

3   A family connection: Chatsworth and Burghley

Talman's entry into the big stakes was marked by his summons to Chatsworth[26] in Derbyshire by the 4th Earl of Devonshire to consult on the rebuilding of the house. He was there around Christmas 1686 and demolition of the old south front followed soon after. Basically Talman's mandate was to rebuild the Elizabethan courtyard house progressively beginning with the south and east fronts. There is no evidence, however, that he produced a comprehensive plan; indeed, the Earl was indecisive and must always have known that money would not be available for ambitious designs. The importance of the east front was that it basically masked the new hall on the inner side of the courtyard, which was begun first, but the front itself followed the rebuilding of its neighbour on the south. As a piece of architecture the east front is a weak companion to the drama and assertiveness next door. Even thinking the worst of Talman he could hardly have commended the juxtaposition. It is better to dwell upon the south front (Plate 22) as a demonstration of his statement and language for the baroque country house. Much has been made of the omnipresence of Bernini's engraved designs for the Louvre, too much in fact, for although the engravings were possessed by Talman, apart from sharing similarities of a massive block-like balustraded elevation, there is little else in common. As would have been expected of Talman, the inquiring browser through volumes of prints, he opened his *Grand Marot* and turned to Le Vau's Vaux le Vicompte and then looked at Antoine Le Pautre's *Les oeuvres d'architecture* for theoretical designs for châteaux. Nothing like Chatsworth had appeared in English architecture, although it is tempting to

28

believe that Talman had seen the 1st Duke of Newcastle's Nottingham Castle begun in 1674 – a crude restatement of Michelangelo's Capitol in Rome. Also relevant is the troubled building history of Thoresby (Plate 23), also in Nottingham-shire,[27] for when that house was being remodelled for the 4th Earl of Kingston between 1685 and 1687, the craftsmen employed – Goudge, Cibber, Verrio, Laguerre, Nost, and Benjamin Jackson – were all to move on as Talman's team at Chatsworth within the following few years. The most that can be said for Thoresby is that it comes out of the Office of Works stable and was central to the parapeted brick and stone-coigned style of Wren's Hampton Court Palace from 1688.

Perplexing also is the authorship of Chatsworth's west front. Talman must have designed the west terrace and stairs (Plate 24) before his dismissal after midsummer 1696, for nothing could be more Talmanic, and sculptural embellishments and masques are derived from the engravings of Charmeton, then in Talman's collection and today at Chatsworth. It is inconceivable that he did not form some design for the intended front, but he never claimed this, and the front as it stands is clearly adaptive to the style of the south front. Fortunately the state apartments (Plates 25–27) in the south front, as well as Chapel and the Hall were completed before Talman made his exit. Now that Cassiobury has gone and most of May's apartments at Windsor, only here and at Burghley is it possible to experience the real high-water mark of a suite of state apartments, not perhaps as grand as St George's Hall and Chapel at Windsor, but containing the same decorative ingredients: painted ceilings, the most masterful and highest quality carved woodwork, intarsia work, gilt and bronze ironwork, and superbly cut and sculptured marble and stone. The baroque effect was increased by the introduction of spatial episodes formed by columnar or arched screens and complicated stairs within painted staircases. Burghley cannot be disassociated from all this, for it is part of the same family patronage. The Countess of Exeter, wife of the 5th Earl, was Lord Devonshire's sister. Talman's presence at Burghley in August and September 1688, coinciding with the redecoration of the interior of this Elizabethan mansion, and a payment in 1704 to him of £200 by the Earl's trustees, is proof of his responsibility for the sumptuous interiors (Plates 28–29) which conform exactly to the Chatsworth style. Once again both Verrio and Gibbons and his followers provided a rich feast where walls and ceilings glow with colour in contrast to the muted and sombre exteriors of the house.

4 The Comptrollership of the Works

The Comptrollership of the Works[28] had been held by Hugh May until his death in 1684; but being then something of an anomaly, for it was essentially administrative and concerned with accountancy, it was not a post with clearly defined functions, and may well have been specially recreated for Talman because of the impending great works at Hampton Court. Indeed, looming behind is the grey eminence of Talman's powerful patron the Earl of Portland. Talman's position at Hampton Court was a very special one incurring enmity, and Reynolds's comment apropos Sir William Chambers and the Royal Academy could have been made by Wren of Talman: 'that though he was President, Sir Wm was Viceroy over him.' Under Portland Talman enjoyed a status that enabled him to command the works in the gardens, in words applied to Portland's commission, 'to oversee and direct any plantations and works therein', and, in effect, although Talman was Comptroller of the Gardens, he was also effectively Portland's Deputy working in parallel with George London, the official Deputy. Between 1689 and 1699 more than £88,000 was spent on the gardens. Talman also enjoyed a peculiarly intimate relationship with the King, addressing him in familiar terms as in August 1699 when he wrote to William in Holland: 'we have an abundance of projects if yr Majesty will like them, by several noble Lords that we here call *the critiques.*'[29]

Wren's responsibility for the general lines of Hampton Court is not doubted. He would obviously have preferred his great scheme which envisaged the total rebuilding of the Tudor palace except for the venerated Great Hall, but financial stringencies ruled this out and Wren was forced to resort to the low,

31

unbroken silhouetted, block-like palace as built. To this end there is no reason to suppose that Talman exerted any influence from 1689, although the generic resemblance to Thoresby in miniature cannot be ignored. Both were arranged around a courtyard, both were of brick with stone detailing, and both affected the slab-like, closely fenestrated look. Talman's chance occurred in April 1699 when the King decided to finish the palace after the interim following Queen Mary's death. To complete the great suite of rooms through the south front from the King's Stairs to the Great Bedchamber and Gallery around the corner on the east front, Talman's, not Wren's, estimate was accepted, and this suite of rooms ought surely to be regarded as a demonstration of Talman's style for interiors. It is significant that none of the pre-1689 designs for decoration were executed in the post-1699 works. The rooms accord well with Talman's concurrent interiors at Chatsworth or at Burghley, and John Nost's chimney in the Gallery, for example, is one resembling Talman's in a Trianon section. Wren must have regarded Talman's dominance from 1699 to 1702 bitterly. There was a row due to the collapse of part of the building in December 1689 from which Wren cannot be entirely absolved causing the death of two carpenters. It was Talman's unfriendly attitude to his chief during the inquiry that exposed his malicious character and made him out to be, as he clearly was, covetous of Wren's position. Talman was a man unable to depute easily, and for this reason a personal quality exists in all his works. Wren, on the other hand, by virtue of his vast responsibilities, not the least with St Paul's Cathedral and the City churches, was the great deputer. Talman would have preferred to have had the sole and autocratic charge of Hampton Court.

5   The maverick style

The idiosyncracies that imbue Talman's work and award him the epithet of maverick can be recognised in a sequence of works from *c.* 1695 to *c.* 1710 embracing Dyrham in Gloucestershire; Waldershare in Kent; Appuldurcome in the Isle of Wight; Dorchester House, Surrey; Drayton House, Northamptonshire; and Witham Park in Somerset. They can also be discerned throughout the many Trianon designs and those commissioned by the Duke of Newcastle. The style is also implicit in the rough sketches of Castle Howard in Yorkshire. At Dyrham Talman found that the west front, though not very spectacular, had already been built by a Samuel Houduroy in 1692. This somewhat restrained Talman's operations, but it determined the parapeted style. In general conformation this front provided Talman with an outline, but he made his front (Plate 30) higher and more lively in ornamentation. The windows were all linked vertically – a French conceit – in fact the whole feeling is a French one, as if he has been looking through his *Grand Marot*, picking up ideas here and there. Typical Talmanic quirks are the inexplicable Jacobean strapwork reliefs above the first floor windows. To the south extends the masculine orangery (Plate 31), the Versailles orangery in miniature, and Talman executes a nice balance on the north end by repeating three bays of the same elevational design, pushing it into the side of the hill. The similarity between this orangery and the chapel at Bretby in Derbyshire is visual stylistic proof that Talman was the architect there, as was, of course, George London as gardener. Talman's work for William Blathwayte at Dyrham began in 1699, and had William III not died and the political scene changed and Blathwayte run out of funds, much more might have been done, for Talman's minimal interiors are almost chaste in their simplicity.

33

Waldershare is one of our unsung houses. Despite gutting by fire in 1913, it was faithfully restored by Sir Reginald Blomfield. Sir Henry Furnese bought the estate in 1705 and is reputed to have built the house by 1712. The garden front (Plate 32) is a rich stone and brick evocation of Hampton Court with a five-bay centre-piece almost smothered in carved stonework and locked in by giant pilasters. Hampton Court is recalled again by the window above the door, a variant of those in the Fountain Court. Somehow this all speaks of Talman, and Talmanic too is the baroque doorway below it with a flattened shell head and dropped ears to the architrave. The whole design of this centre part is subtle, for the pilasters, doubled at the outer ends, and the entablature form as it were a framework in which the voids are given prominence. The two outer bays at either side of this centre-piece are more simply detailed and this is marked by the angle pilasters which are strips, not an order. Then there are even simpler astylar lower extensions, and lower still single storey wings pushing forward. This was clearly the show front for the garden. On the entrance front (Plate 33) simplicity was again the keynote with the three-bay centre projecting slightly and marked off by pilaster strips. From this angle the huge laterally placed chimney-stacks can be seen, rising to a linking arch. If Waldershare is by Talman – and its garden (Plate 34) was in London's style – then so surely is Appuldurcombe (Plate 35), for the five-bay centre of one is but a restatement of the other; all the cards in the pack are the same, and just as the doorway at Waldershare belongs to the same vocabulary as the voids on the rejected Newcastle designs, so are Appuldurcombe's windows set against a wall of horizontal channelled stonework. Appuldurcombe was built for Sir Robert Worsley from *c.*1701 and has been attributed to John James without any conclusive evidence[30] that he was acting in an architectural capacity. If any architect was responsible for this wayward house it was surely Talman. It possesses a nonconformist disrespect for the conventional that with a lesser architect could be a weakness.

With Talman it is a virtue and produced fronts or elevations which charm by their difference from anything else. Such a one was the garden front of Dorchester House, a huge and conventional hipped-roof house built for the 6th Duke of Norfolk *c.* 1675. For Sir David Colyear, one of the king's soldiers (commemorated by magnificent gate trophies, Plate 38) created Earl of Portmore in 1703, Talman added a block-like extension to the garden front with a felicitous arrangement of arched voids (Plates 36–37) with single-bay towers terminated by cupolas. It was an extraordinarily novel design that accords well with the unconventionality of Vanbrugh's little houses. The allusion of the tall towers demarcating the boundaries of the front to those at Drayton, which frame the scene for the visitor unaware of the delights of the courtyard to come, are obvious.

The appeal of Drayton lies in the manner in which Talman introduced an ornamental liveliness to the south front (Plate 39) facing a courtyard of restricted extent, yet at the same time monumental. His contract with Sir John Germaine is dated 1702; although Talman was certainly the executant architect, serious consideration ought to be given to the possibility that he gave the task of designing it to John, whose elevation (Plate 40) for one of his Trianon projects is so similar. The influences that bear upon Drayton are as much Genoese as anything else, although not necessarily from Rubens's *Palazzi di Genova* as from the Witt Grisoni-Talman sketch-book. There is nothing in English architecture quite like Drayton and for that it can be celebrated, and is Talman's strength. It might have been likewise at Witham, for there Sir William Wyndham presented him with the problem[31] of remodelling an old house set around three sides of a courtyard. The problem might have been solved conventionally, but Talman conceived the idea of screening the fourth side with a transparent portico (Plates 41–42). The dating is undecided although Talman's design was included by Colen Campbell in the second volume of *Vitruvius Britannicus* (1717) whilst in manuscript, but was discarded for Gibbs's version when printed. So up to 1716 Talman's project was still in being. Admittedly Drayton and Witham are minor episodes. Castle Howard, the Trianon and the Duke of Newcastle's projects would have been great achievements had they not remained paper dreams.

Castle Howard preceded the Trianon as an exposure of Talman's ideas. The 3rd Earl of Carlisle had summoned Talman to Castle Howard in anticipation of building grandly. It was not to be for 'Captain' Vanbrugh, the soldier and playwright, ousted Talman, so evoking that remark by Swift that 'Van's genius, without thought or lecture, is hugely turn'd to architecture.' With Talman came his inevitable counterpart, George London, whose survey plan provides a hint as to the unconventionality of at least one scheme. Two plans basically propose palace-like blocks, a fifteen-by-five bay one (Plate 43)[32] with pilaster porticoes and pilasters demarcating the end bays, and (Plate 44) a thirteen-by-six bay block, astylar this time, and with a huge oval saloon in the manner of the Château de Turny from the *Grand Marot*, identified as projecting from the centre by a partly curved, partly canted bay. Both designs possess complex stairs that reappear in the Newcastle projects. On the back of the 'Turny' plan is a precious little sketch (Plate 45) as evidence for a different sort of solution for a house around three sides of a courtyard and opening out on the court side to a baroque forecourt arrangement with pavilions and quadrant wings and concavo-convex walls. One of the 'Trianon' sketch-leaves (Plate 46) may be for Castle Howard as plans on it relate as much to the inscribed conventional ones as to the Trianon. If so, then the rough elevational studies convey some idea of its external style: the sombre block-like silhouette of Chatsworth spelt out in a richer and enlivened vocabulary. The ground floor is rusticated, pierced by arched windows; the piano-nobile windows above have emphatic balconies, and above them are blank roundels with busts. Obviously the stylistic aspirations at Castle Howard were concurrent with those for the Trianon.

The idea of a retreat for the King away from the formalities of Hampton Court may have germinated about 1698 and belong to the 'abundance of projects' mentioned by Talman to the King in August 1699.[33] Like Castle Howard, Talman first drew out a conservative palace-like block (Plate 47) with Talmanic stair arrangements and a vaulted underhall supporting a forty-by-forty foot entrance hall above. At this stage no decision had necessarily been made that the Trianon was to be sited on the other side of the Thames near Thames Ditton – in fact roughly on the site of the present Surbiton station. A sheet of studies (Plate 48) of remarkable neo-Palladian, or more properly neo-Gibbsian, designs then followed, at least two resembling houses in Gibbs's *Book of Architecture* of 1728.[34] Associated sketch-book leaves (Plates 49–50) show an increasing idiosyncracy of invention with studies for pavilions or lodges, temples or garden layouts, with one charming, petite house which could be a design for George London's house at Thames Ditton. Many of the preliminary plans (Plates 51–52) are expressed externally in the most articulate way with breaks, niches, apsed loggias, pavilions at the angles, and columnar episodes, germinating in Talman's mind right back to the days of Hackwood. Finally Talman settled upon two schemes both of which were carefully drawn out: a penultimate one which might be described as Italianate – Roman with French undertones – with an entrance (Plates 53–54) based upon St Maria in Via Lata fronting a circular loggia that was divided by a narrow vestibule from the stairs winding round a circular staircase marked externally by a dome. This project is seen in section across the width of the garden bounded by small, domed tempiettos, thus revealing it to be a substitute for the 'final' scheme (Plates 55–56) drawn to the same scale but now in what could be called a *Grand Marot* style with interiors (Plate 56) laced by Dutch baroque details from Justus Danckerts's *Architectura Civilis* with its chimney-pieces by Bullet, and reflecting also Talman's own acquaintance with Daniel Marot.

The effect would have been richly ornamental and sculptural with a niched and columned loggia spatially and plastically opening into the oval hall (Plate 57), a device that had first been experimented with in the Bond plan (Plate 18) of 1688 and would again feature in the Newcastle projects. Had the King not died in 1702 this Trianon might have arisen across the river, and Talman would have needed no monograph for one would have long since been written. It is also proof that Talman enjoyed a peculiarly intimate relationship with the King, which may possibly have had something to do with the backing of his Dutch courtier friends and patrons. After William's death Talman was, in effect, in retreat, and this was the position with the Newcastle fiasco where the conniving Vanbrugh may have defeated him, but did not succeed either.

Had the Castle Howard elevations survived some must certainly have matched those multitudinous ones offered to John Holles, Duke of Newcastle, in 1702–3, and perhaps also

resembled the 'Great' design (Plate 58) for Kimberley submitted
c. 1701. The Duke was indecisive whether to rebuild his ancient
seat at Welbeck or a minor one at Haughton, both in Nottinghamshire. One set of three designs is inscribed for Haughton, the
others could be for either house. Once again there are conventional plans, one (Plate 59) in a formal London-like garden;
then there are two elevations of similar size both with equally
scaled storeys above a low basement. The principal element of
one (Plate 60) is a pilaster portico and a flat balustraded roof; the
other (Plate 61) is much more frenchified with a two-storey
Grand Marot frontispiece and a hipped roof with baroque
windows, and in the treatment of the pavilions there is a little of
Hooke's Bethlehem Hospital. Perhaps for Welbeck Talman then
conceived two schemes. In one (Plates 62–65) the fenestration is
of a plainer, conventional sort, but interest is given to the
exteriors by the advance and recession of the plan. The angles are
capped by baroque domes, and the frontispieces – one superimposed on the other with a giant pilastered order against a
channelled face – are topped with Drayton-like raised
pedimented panels with side scrolled volutes. This project is then
dressed up (Plate 66) with windows from Rossi's recently
published *Studio d'Architettura Civile*, a more emphatic use of
coigning, and wall facings of horizontal, channelled-cut stone;
and on one design this stone face pierced by windows is strongly
reminiscent of the almost concurrent Appuldurcombe. Talman's
pavilion elevation would not have been alien to Turin and the
general vocabulary of this scheme is of the Roman-trained
Thomas Archer and his Heythrop, Oxfordshire, begun in 1707.
It was all very novel, and novel too was the Haughton project, a
site plan (Plate 67) showing Talman's prophetic use of a main
block linked at the four angles by quadrant colonnades to
outstanding office blocks; a plan (Plate 68) that starts off as an
idea from the old Duke of Newcastle's Nottingham Castle, but is
given spatial excitement by an Italianate palazzo-type stair rising
up through a huge hall from a double screen of columns, as in the
Welbeck plan (Plate 63); and an elevation (Plate 69) that
introduces for the first (and last?) time to English architecture
after John Webb the palazzo block with superimposed orders,
and drawing upon details in Rossi. The Roman quality of this

design is underlined by a rough sketch on the verso of the drawing showing (Plate 70) an idea for a typical Roman saloon or hall with an oval relief set above the chimney-piece.

The part played by Vanbrugh in Talman's downfall[35] with the Duke reveals a nasty side of his nature that conflicts with the usual picture of amicability and perhaps cancels out Talman's own vexatious character. It may be true that the Duke was probably playing off one architect against the other, but not at all proven that Talman had been redrawing Vanbrugh's own designs; indeed, it may be the other way round. In April 1703 Talman had had to confess to the Duke an outline of his lawsuit with Lord Carlisle, and when Vanbrugh got wind of this he laid into Talman with a vengeance, but in so doing compiled that invaluable list of those patrons who had 'met with vexations'. Had he not done so we would not have known of Talman's concerns with Lady Falkland, probably at Knebworth in Hertfordshire, with Lord Normanby at Buckingham House, Lord Portmore at Dorchester House, and Lord Coningsby at Hampton Court in Herefordshire. Perhaps, as Vanbrugh wrote, they all had 'the vexation of stumbling in the same hole', but it is doubtful that even he would not have denied that Talman gave his clients good houses, had dominated the country house circuit for nearly twenty years, and had stamped his idiosyncracies upon almost everything he built. Talman was an ideas man, and it is in the fertility of his ideas that he occupies so prominent a place in the development and typology of country house design under William III. For the following twenty years almost every architect of consequence inherited something from Talman and that is surely not a bad record.

6   Astylar austerity

The sheet of sketches for a Trianon (Plate 48) that incorporates a design for a remarkable rotunda, includes also four studies for exteriors, in a decidedly proto-neo-Palladian mood for a date roughly between 1698 and 1702. They lack Talman's usual ornamental brio and could have been used by John James in 1711 to demonstrate 'that the Beautys of Architecture may consist with the greatest Plainess of the structure.' It is surely a mark of Talman's wondrous adaptiveness, or even inconsistency, that he was able and perfectly willing to pursue an architectural theme diametrically opposed to his maverick style. The fact that examples of this plain style occur late in his career suggests that he may have sought to enlarge his repertoire. It would be tempting, but hazardous, to associate the Trianon sketches with Talman's possession of the Palladio drawings. His new style which is austere and astylar can be illustrated by Kimberley Hall in Norfolk, Fetcham Park in Surrey, and Panton Hall, Lincolnshire.

The first document in this sequence beginning with Kimberley is a land survey (Plate 71) made about 1700 for Sir John Wodehouse. It may be an old survey, but it is marked with dots for proposed avenues and is suspiciously like George London's method. On this has been featured the 'New House design'd to be Built',[36] a vast mansion with slightly projecting wings and centre and with big, square, lateral courtyards. The scale is obviously that of Castle Howard, and the way in which offices are developed around courtyards they are clearly intended to be visually integral with the body of the house – a parallel development with Vanbrugh and Hawksmoor. The dating of this is obviously important, but a clue is contained in Sir John Wodehouse's bank account at Hoare's under 27 March 1701 where Talman was paid £58.15.[37] This 'Great' plan was succeeded by a quite different one, a pavilion plan (Plate 72) in which the pavilions were contained within the body of the house and only identified externally by shallow breaks. This plan was also discarded, but Kimberley as built (Plate 73) followed more or less the arrangement of the nine-bay centre, 3–3–3 bays, with a two-and-a-half storey elevation and pediment. A new spirit has entered English architecture, an austerity expressed with the very plainest of exteriors and relying for its effect upon refined brickwork and a subtle and careful balance between wall and voids. This astylism has always been recognised as an achievement by Gibbs after 1720.

From 1705 Talman was building a similar house (Plate 74) for Arthur Moore, a South Sea Company director, at Fetcham near Leatherhead. Moore's house was almost identical in size and treatment except that the window rhythm was changed from 3–3–3 to 4–3–4. Whereas Kimberley had been relatively unchanged outside except for the unusual decision *c.* 1755 to reinstate Talman's intended towers,[38] but redecorated inside except for some cross-vaulted corridors, Fetcham has been grossly rebuilt externally with French pavilion roofs, preserving, however, a splendid painted staircase (Plate 75). It is by Louis Laguerre, the painter of the one in Buckingham House, and is a restatement of that stair-hall arrangement with the deliberate juxtaposition of low, dark hall and high, light, painted staircase.

Both Kimberley and Fetcham would have been isolated examples of this austere style had it not been for the demolition of Panton Hall (Plate 76) in 1960. This revealed the earlier house (Plate 77) and demonstrated that John Carr only added lateral extensions for Edmund Turnor in 1775, carefully copying the fine brickwork and adding canted bays to the ends that repeat the earlier one on the garden front. The original house can therefore be reconstructed as 2–3–2 bays on the north entrance front, and on the south garden front with the three-bay centre expressed as a canted bay answering an oval-ended saloon behind leading off an oblong entrance hall – an exact repetition of the centre arrangement of Talman's Castle Howard plan (Plate 44). The demolition also revealed some evidence for columnar screening, rebuilt by Carr, between the hall and one of the adjacent rooms.

41

The house was built of the same fine, smooth red brick as Kimberley and being of four storeys was unusually tall. When William Angus compiled his *Seats of the Nobility and Gentry* in 1787 he ascribed Panton to Hawksmoor, writing that Joseph Gace had built it about 1720. Panton is naturally quite atypical of Hawksmoor, but not of Talman, whose involvement was revealed to the late Dr Margaret Whinney in 1955 by a Dr Hurst who claimed to have been shown Talman's designs for the house when he stayed there with the Turnor family before the war. Panton was probably being built when Talman died in 1719 and Gace must have secured the advice of Hawksmoor in the completion.

In the consideration of these three astylar houses, Gibbs as the inheritor of the style cannot be doubted. Throughout Talman's late career, and through probable contacts between Gibbs and John Talman, there are many strange tie-ups that would suggest a more intimate professional relationship between them than the evidence would suggest.

7 Architect and gardener: Talman and London

The role of the architect as partner with the gardener has never been studied. Gardens of the first Stuart Court by the likes of Isaac de Caus were architectural ensembles with gateways, gazeboes, arbours, arcaded terrace works, grottoes and even triumphal arches. De Caus appears to have managed all this himself, for he combined the talents of architect and gardener. Inigo Jones never designed a garden, but was fond of garden gateways and built many. By the early eighteenth century the architect had almost usurped the gardener. There is not a scrap of evidence that Charles Bridgeman designed any of the architectural episodes in his gardens. He would propose a plan, arrange the terraces, mounts and amphitheatres, but the architect generally added the buildings. For example, all the buildings at Eastbury or Stowe are by Vanbrugh. Later, Sir William Chambers at Kew Gardens was probably the last of the architect-gardeners, and significantly he was succeeded by Capability Brown who played the same role as de Caus, combining the professions of gardener and architect.

The relationship between George London and William Talman was undoubtedly one of close collaboration. It is therefore rewarding to speculate on the extent to which London may have summoned Talman to design those architectural parts of his gardens. Generally, where Talman goes, London follows, or vice versa. At Chatsworth, Burghley, Castle Ashby, Dyrham, Castle Howard, Hampton Court, Middlesex as well as Hampton Court in Herefordshire, probably Kimberley and Fetcham, and possibly at Lord Clarendon's Cornbury, the chief architect and gardener of the Williamite Court were together. It would be

43

irresponsible to deny London the ability to design garden buildings. Nevertheless, apart from sculptural works such as fountains, and minor architectural embellishments, Talman the architect intervenes to design the major architectural episodes in a London garden. Hence at Chatsworth in 1693 Talman designed the splendid bowling green temple (Plate 78) adjacent to the west parterre (Plate 79) that London had contracted for in 1690, and Talman's is almost certainly the greenhouse (Plate 80) of 1697 even if it was built after his dismissal. At Castle Ashby, Northamptonshire, concurrent with an unexecuted contract for remodelling the north front for the 4th Earl of Northampton in 1695, London was present too, and Talman's must certainly be the attractive greenhouse (Plate 81), now mostly demolished, with its baroque attic and pineapple finials. At Dyrham Talman's orangery was designed as an extension of the house, and although London designed most of the garden, the existence of a baroque design (Plate 82) for a combination of cascade and stairs flowing from a terrace demonstrates how much Talman was concerned with the architectural arrangements. The orangery here so resembles the chapel at Bretby (Plate 83) in Derbyshire as to merit an attribution. Here the Earl of Chesterfield had rebuilt his Jacobean house by the 1670s, but what Knyff's engraved view shows is the state of the gardens by *c.* 1700 when a second phase of works had been completed from the late 1680s. The pavilion to the cross-wing is in a full-blooded French Le Vau style, but it is not known if it belongs to some post-fire works of the 1680s which were almost certainly by London. The presence of Mr Grillet, an hydraulics engineer, who was working at Chatsworth adds strength to the Talman-London connection. These new garden works included the greenhouse and the extension of the gardens down into the valley with architecturally ornamented terraces. Three other large greenhouses in George London gardens which bear the stamp of Talmans style are Lord Ferrers' at Staunton Harold, Leicestershire (Plate 84), Lord Ossulton's at Dawley in Middlesex (Plate 85) and Lord Radnor's at Wimpole in Cambridgeshire (Plate 86), all of the 1690s. It is also tempting to attribute to Talman the little garden loggia (Plate 87) at Kensington Palace that may belong to garden works carried out during the last years of the King's reign under London's partner

Henry Wise and possibly concurrent with Talman's payment of £131 (to Wren's £92) for 'looking after said New Building K. Palace July 1700.'[39] The loggia recalls the later Queen Anne's Walk at Barnstaple (Plate 88) built for Robert Rolle in 1708. There are echoes here too of the Drayton courtyard colonnades as well as the splendid military trophies on Lord Portmore's gate piers at Dorchester House, Surrey.

At Hampton Court, Middlesex, the respective roles of Wren as Surveyor and Talman as Comptroller often overlap. London laid down the main compartments of the garden: the Privy Garden, the Great Fountain Garden, the Wilderness and the Kitchen Garden. It is not even clear who really built the Bowling Green with its four temples, although both Talman and Hawksmoor made designs, as did an anonymous architect.[40] The abortive projects for the Trianon display a precociousness in the creation of a garden with an abundance of architectural features, and John's own designs are so extravagant that they would have dwarfed many a great continental garden. The analogy with the European garden in the Versailles tradition is obvious in considering one of London's last gardens and his greatest, at Wanstead in Essex, a vast, formal layout on the scale of the first Versailles was laid down from 1706 for Sir Richard Child. The architectural episodes are so Talmanic as to warrant a firm attribution to him, especially the French-roofed pavilion (Plate 89) terminating the terrace by the bowling green, probably the richly ordered bowling green itself, and the greenhouse (Plate 90), the Castle Ashby one writ large. Such a magnificent garden around an old-fashioned house must have been initiated with the idea of building a new one. Whether it was Talman's vexatious character or just his misfortune, when Sir Richard commissioned a new house in 1713 he turned to the inexperienced Colen Campbell, who provided him with the first neo-Palladian great house in England. Wanstead was the death knell of the baroque school of Vanbrugh and Hawksmoor, just as Castle Howard had spelt the end of the Talman dominance.

Notes

1 The debt was naturally earlier, for 1685 was the year judgement was given to Talman against Clarendon, so it is possible that it was incurred in 1683. It doesn't appear to have damaged their relations. According to John Talman's Books (Bodleian Library, MS Eng. Letters e 34; letter of 16 April, 1708) Apprice was married to William's sister.

2 Petition to Edward Harley in 1713 to regain the Comptrollership after the change of government when Vanbrugh had been dismissed; he was, however, reinstated in 1715.

3 See in particular a sale catalogue in Sir John Soane's Museum of 19–24 April 1727. It is probable that quantities of drawings and albums now at Chatsworth came from Talman and ultimately from Inigo Jones. Other located sales are: 2 Feb. 1726 (pre-death); 26 April 1727; 4–10 April 1728; and one following Mrs Talman's death in March 1733. See also Vertue's sales 17–22 March 1757 and sale folders in Gough Collection, Bodleian Library, Oxford.

4 Talman's Probate Inventory is dated 22 December 1719 and was kindly shown to me by Dr Lindsey Boynton and should be published. It conveys a picture of an unusual assemblage of works of art of the richest sort: many carved marble vases, porphyry tables, inlaid columns, capitals, slabs, many sculptures by Duquesnoy, antique marbles and copies after the antique, plasters, bronzes and stands, 'a large Chimney Piece with Slab and Slips all compleat very curious cut out of Greek Marble' and another 'of most rare Marble cut out of some fragment of the Arundel Marble' – and these for some as yet unexplained reason stored or housed in Dr J. T. Desaguilier's house in Channel Row, Westminster. This is added proof that the John Talman section of a room in the Victoria and Albert Museum (3434.246) is precious evidence of their collection in situ.

5 The scarcity of Portland papers to do with his seat at Bulstrode precludes any assessment of Talman's probable involvement. The house had been built for Lord Jeffreys c. 1680 around an earlier one, and this is shown on a land survey in the Buckinghamshire Record Office. Portland's alterations can be seen by comparing this survey with the views by Willson in J. Badeslade and J. Rocque's *Vitruvius Brittanicus, Volume the Fourth*, 1739, pls.40–44. The comparison demonstrates that Portland, as might have been expected, laid out a magnificent formal garden in the manner of George London, possibly employing for the great parterre, Claude Desgots, Le Notre's son-in-law whom Portland had brought over from France. The front to this parterre received stone-terraced stairs at each end, and these are Talmanic.

Notes

6 L. Whistler, *The Imagination of Vanbrugh and his Fellow Artists*, 1954, pp. 34–40.

7 John was abroad on at least three visits: 1699–1702, 1709–16 and 1719.

8 Samuel Gale to William Stukeley, 30 March 1727; *Family Memoirs of the Rev. William Stukeley*, I, 193; *The Surtees Soc.*, V, 73, 1882.

9 MS description of 21 January 1724 by a member of the Spalding Gentlemen's Society (Society MSS).

10 British Museum, Add. MS 14296, f. 62.

11 Bodleian Library, Gough Maps, 10, f. 37.

12 Significantly this is in the Gibbs Collection in the Ashmolean (Gibbs II, 28) and it has the name of Talman crossed out. The rotunda does not necessarily relate to the plan, on which the 'villa' is shown in complete isolation with the offices hidden in a nearby wood and connected by a tunnel.

13 London University, Courtauld Institute of Art. The sketch-book has never been studied but relates to John Talman's 1709–16 travels.

14 At Abbotstone the site of the house can be located as can traces of garden works. The exact extent of Gibbs's involvement is imprecisely known.

15 *Country Life*, 17, 24 May 1913 has a plan which has been drawn to reconstruct the old house within the Wyatt enlargements; see also C. R. Cockerell's plan and description in John Harris, 'Ichnographica Domestica' in *Architectural History*, XIV, 1971 and a survey at Hachwood with the house in perspective.

16 Photographs in National Monuments Record.

17 For de Voorst see Van der Wijct, 'De Voorst' in *Bulletin K.N.O.B.* 1963 and the further discussion in W. Kuyper, *Dutch Classicist Architecture*, 1980.

18 Edward Southwell's Diary: see Katherine Freemantle, 'A visit to the United Provinces and Cleves in the time of William III', in *Nederlands Kunsthistorisch Jaarboek*, 21, 1970.

19 Previously published as by Wren by Sir John Summerson in 'The Classical Country House in Eighteenth-Century England' in *Royal Society of Arts Jnl*, July 1959, 560; but see John Harris, 'Kneller Hall' in *The Country Seat*, ed. H. M. Colvin and John Harris, 1970, plate 54, for an account of Kneller's house at Whitton that could on stylistic grounds be by Talman.

20 *Vitruvius Britannicus*, II, 1717, pls. 35–6.

21 Colvin and Harris, *op cit.*

22 James Gibbs, *Book of Architecture*, 1728, plate 56.

23 J. Dallaway, *Western Division of Sussex*, I, 1815, 158–9, 193.

24 Sir Thomas Bond's second son Thomas married in 1686 the daughter of Lord Jermyn; could also be for the Bonds of Peckham or Bonds at Creech Grange, Dorset.

25 At the same time Clarendon was altering Cornbury where the gardens were under London's management around September 1689.

26 For Chatsworth see Francis Thompson, *A History of Chatsworth*, 1949.

27 For the contorted and inconclusive history of Thoresby see the summing-up in H. M. Colvin, *Dictionary*, 1978. It has never been pointed out how sophisticated the plan is. The stair arrangements are particularly magisterial.

28 For this account I am indebted to *The History of the King's Works*, ed. H. M. Colvin, V, 1976: period 1660–1782.

29 Information from J. H. V. Davies.

30 The basic evidence for James's participation is contained in L. O. J. Boynton, *Appuldurcombe House*, 1967. One piece of evidence for his involvement is that Worsley's brother-in-law, Lord Weymouth, was quoted in a list of 'Persons of Quality' to vouch for James's skill in building. This list is long and includes both noblemen and commoners. It seems incredible that in 1711 the list did not include Worsley; and, of course, if Appuldurcombe and Waldershare are by the same architects, Furnese as well. I think this is damning proof that James was not the architect of Appuldurcombe, but probably the master carpenter, or else, and this should not be discredited, completed the house after Talman had either been dismissed or for some other reason was not willing to superintend a house so inaccessible.

31 The dating of Witham is imprecise. Many designs were made for the rebuilding and these are published by H. M. Colvin in his *Catalogue of Architectural Drawings in Worcester College Library*, 1964 – by Hawksmoor, Thornhill and George Clarke. It is not even clear if the Gibbs house was built; but see John Harris, 'The Transparent Portico' in *Arch. Rev.*, CXXVIII, 1958, 108–9.

32 The connection in planning between this block-like house and J. Von Bodt's Beningborough, Yorkshire, is a little uncanny. Bodt may have made his design *c.* 1710; both Gibbs and Archer appear to have been involved; see John Harris, 'Bodt and Stainbrough' in *Arch. Rev.*, July 1961.

33 See note 29 for information.

34 James Gibbs, *Book of Architecture*, 1728, pls. 55 and 59.

35 Whistler, *op cit.*

36 *Cf.* comparable London avenues drawn on the 1649 survey of Wotton House, Buckinghamshire; information from Dr George Clarke.

37 Information from Dr Timothy Connor.

38 This reinstatement was carried out by Thomas Prowse with the assistance of John Sanderson *c.* 1755; it is not known if they were aware of Talman's first designs.

39 Information from Mr J. H. V. Davies who quite rightly questioned the extent of Talman's role here.

40 Wren Society IV, 1927, pls. XXV–XXVII; possibly these three designs in Sir John Soane's Museum *are* by Talman, as they relate in plan to RIBA G2/26$^{1-2}$, a building on a larger scale.

List of documented and attributed works

HACKWOOD PARK, HAMPSHIRE, new house for 6th Marquess of Winchester, 1683. *Attributed*

ABBOTSTONE, HAMPSHIRE, hunting lodge for 6th Marquess of Winchester, 1683. *Attributed*

BLYTH HALL, NOTTINGHAMSHIRE, new house for Edward Mellish, 1683. *Attributed*

LONDON, ST ANNE'S CHURCH, SOHO, 1685. Completion with Wren; design for steeple, 1714.

STANSTEAD PARK, SUSSEX, new house for 1st Earl of Scarborough, 1686. *Uncertain attribution*

CHATSWORTH HOUSE, DERBYSHIRE, east and south fronts and garden works for 4th Earl of Devonshire, 1687–96.

MR BOND, design for unlocated house, 1688.

BURGHLEY HOUSE, NORTHAMPTONSHIRE, interiors for 5th Earl of Exeter, 1688 and probably from 1682.

SWALLOWFIELD HOUSE, BERKSHIRE, new house for 2nd Earl of Clarendon, 1689.

CORNBURY HOUSE, OXFORDSHIRE, alterations for 2nd Earl of Clarendon, 1689. *Attributed*

BRETBY HALL, DERBYSHIRE, possible rebuilding of cross wings, chapel and garden, for Earl of Chesterfield, *c.* 1690. *Attributed*

UPPARK, SUSSEX, new house for Lord Grey, *c.* 1690. *Uncertain attribution*

BULSTRODE PARK, BUCKINGHAMSHIRE, alterations and terraces for 1st Earl of Portland, *c.* 1690. *Attributed*

LOWTHER HALL, WESTMORLAND, advice on new house for Sir John Lowther, 1692.

CAMBRIDGE, ST CATHERINE'S COLLEGE, chapel, 1694.

DE VOORST, HOLLAND, new house for Earl of Albemarle, 1695.

CASTLE ASHBY, NORTHAMPTONSHIRE, greenhouse for 4th Earl of Northampton, *c.* 1695.

HAMPTON COURT, HEREFORDSHIRE, rebuilding and restoration works and gardens for Lord Coningsby, *c.* 1696.

KINETON PARK, YORKSHIRE, supplied design *c.* 1697, probably not involved in house as built.

DYRHAM PARK, GLOUCESTERSHIRE, east front, etc. for William Blathwayte, 1698.

CASTLE HOWARD, YORKSHIRE, unexecuted designs for 3rd Earl of Carlisle, 1698.

HAMPTON COURT PALACE, MIDDLESEX, completion of state apartments for William III, 1699.

KNEBWORTH, HERTFORDSHIRE, hall range for Lady Falkland, *c.* 1700. *Attributed*

THAMES DITTON, SURREY, small house for George London, *c.* 1700, *Attributed*

LONDON, KENSINGTON PALACE, garden loggia and undefined works, for William III, *c.* 1699. *Attributed*

DORCHESTER HOUSE, SURREY, new garden front, etc., for 1st Earl of Portmore, *c.* 1700.

FETCHAM PARK, SURREY, new house for Arthur Moore, *c.* 1700.

HERRIARD PARK, HAMPSHIRE, unexecuted designs for Thomas Jervoise, *c.* 1700.

KIMBERLEY PARK, NORFOLK, new house for Sir John Wodehouse, *c.* 1700.

APPULDURCOMBE, ISLE OF WIGHT, new house for Sir Richard Worsley, *c.* 1701. *Attributed*

DRAYTON HOUSE, NORTHAMPTONSHIRE, south front, etc. for Sir John Germaine, 1702.

WELBECK ABBEY and HAUGHTON HOUSE, NOTTINGHAMSHIRE, unexecuted designs for new house for 1st Duke of Newcastle, 1703.

WALDERSHARE PARK, KENT, new house for Sir Robert Furness, 1705. *Attributed*

WANSTEAD HOUSE, ESSEX, garden works for Sir Richard Child, 1706. *Attributed*

BARNSTAPLE, QUEEN ANNE'S WALK, for Robert Rolle, 1708. *Attributed*

CANNONS HOUSE, MIDDLESEX, offices for 1st Duke of Chandos, 1713.

PANTON HALL, LINCOLNSHIRE, new house for Joseph Gace, *c.* 1719, completed by Hawksmoor.

Select bibliography

F. B. Benger, 'Fetcham Park', in *Proceedings of the Leatherhead and District Local History Society*, vol. 2, no. 1, 1957.

H. M. Colvin, *A Biographical Dictionary of British Architects, 1600–1840*, 1978, as a source for all literary references to individual buildings except for Benger and Saunders.

Kerry Downes, *English Baroque Architecture*, 1966.

John Harris, 'The Hampton Court Trianon Designs of William and John Talman', in *Journal of the Warburg and Courtauld Institutes*, xxiii, 1960.

Edward Saunders, 'Bretby Hall', in *Derbyshire Life*, August, 1975.

M. D. Whinney, 'William Talman', in *Journal of the Warburg and Courtauld Institutes*, xviii, 1955.

Index

PLATES

Portrait of Talman probably in his fifties; therefore after 1700. Not an attractive cast of mouth!

2. Plan of a house by John Talman *c.* 1702: an ideal for the Talman family seat, perhaps in Norfolk though possibly at Thames Ditton.

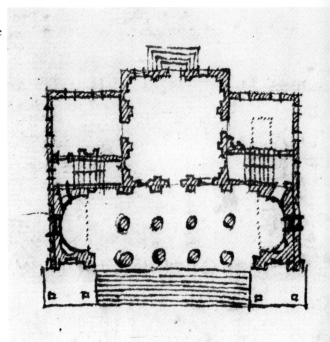

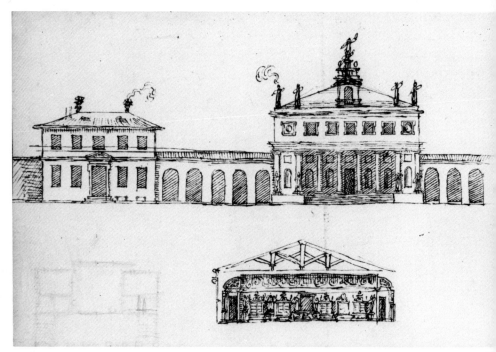

3. A part elevation and section through the library of the Talman family seat; of indeterminate date. A custom-designed library with architecturally designed bookcases, anticipating the interiors of William Kent in the 1720s and 1730s.

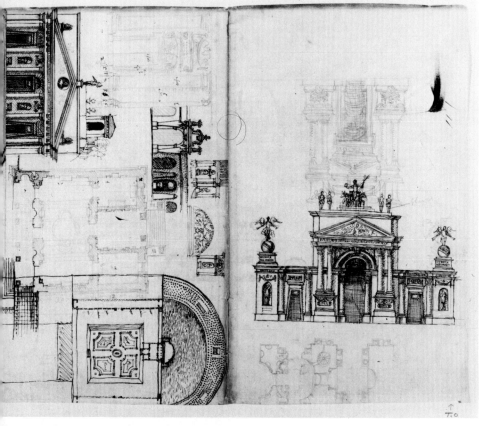

…n extraordinary group of studies that must relate to John Talman's ideas for a Trianon at Hampton …rt, although there is evidence that he played with ideas for a new Palace of Whitehall.

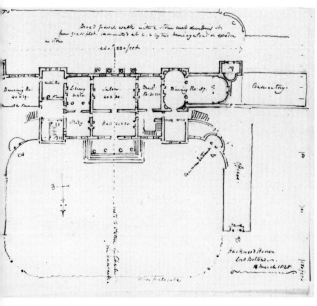

5. When C.R. Cockerell went to Hackwood Park, Hampshire, in 1825 it was in the process of being rebuilt. His plan reveals the character of the first house attributed to William Talman.

6. One of the excellent ceilings remaining at Hackwood in the style of Edward Goudge, whom Talman was probably employing then, and by the same plasterer of the ceiling over the staircase at Blyth Hall

The pear-wood model for the Château de Voorst. English in style it was almost certainly designed by
[Tal]man for William III's favourite. It was paid for by the King and built by Dutch architects, modified
[to t]heir tastes.

[J]ames Gibbs's Kelmarsh Hall, Northamptonshire, is contrasted here with de Voorst to show the
[pri]macy of Talman's influence.

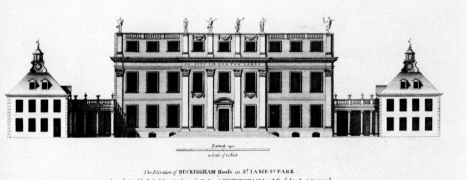

[B]uckingham House, London, engraved in 1715. A major advance in country house design, it was
[en]ormously influential because of its urban and pivotal situation in St James's Park.

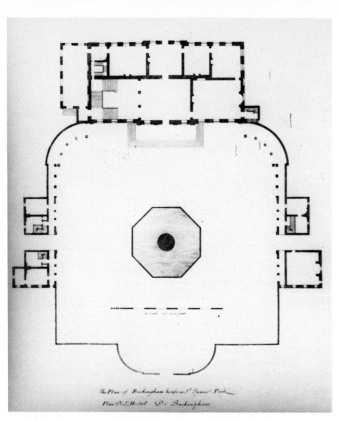

The Plan of Buckingham house in St. James' Park

Plan D: L'Hotel De Buckingham

10. (left) Buckingham House, London; the plan showing the relationship of entrance hall stairs. The low dark hall and high light painted stairs are by Louis Laguerre, who painted the same arrangement of hall and stairs at Fetcham Park, Surrey, for Talman c. 1705.

11. (below) Talman's rather fashioned design for a house for the Earl of Devonshire in Lamb's Conduit Fields. The plan was made before 1694 and is curious because it contains none of his usual idiosyncrat episodes.

12. (right) Blyth Hall, Nottinghamshire, shown here not long before its demolition Begun in 1683 it was prophetic of the neo-Palladian tower house. The upper parts of the towers have been rebuilt, so it uncertain how they were treated.

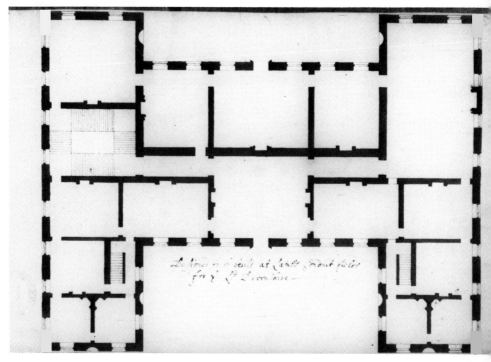

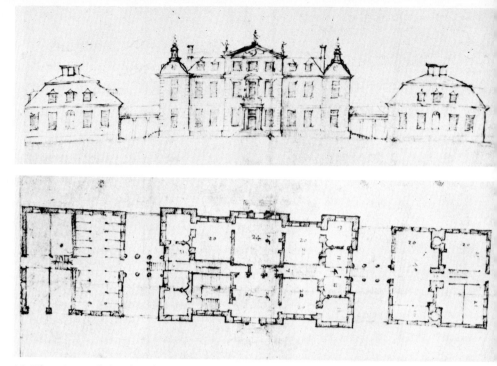

13. Elevation and plan for a house often attributed to Wren, but certainly by Talman and possessing typical Talmanic features, notably the placing of the stairs in the spine of the house, each side of the hall.

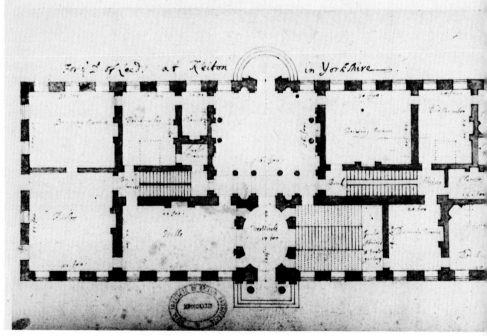

14. Kiveton House, Yorkshire, with its spatially fluid arrangement of oval hall and stairs. There are stairs also in the spine and the gallery across one side of the hall or saloon.

5. Uppark in Sussex has the edge on Stanstead as a potential Talman house, from the stylistic point of
view. The garden is highly sophisticated and bespeaks the hand of George London.

16. Stanstead Park, Sussex, is too plain to be by Talman and impossible if he designed Uppark. A mo
likely candidate would be Robert Hooke.

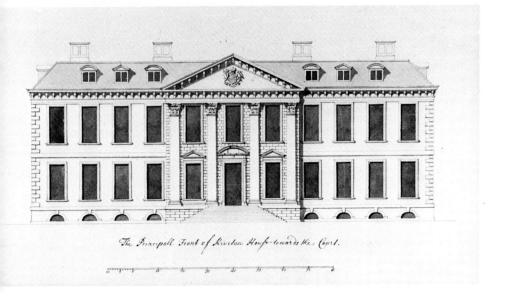

The Principall Front of Kiveton House towards the Court.

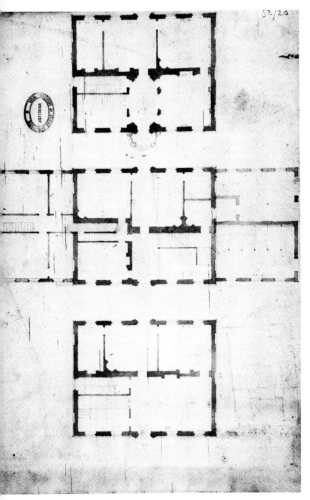

17. (above) This measured drawing of Kiveton House, Yorkshire, seems to have been prepared for James Gibbs, who may have been contemplating its rebuilding. The elevation bears no resemblance to Talman's preliminary plan, but the level of sophistication suggests a London man as designer if not builder.

18. (left) These plans for Mr Bond in 1688 cannot be ascribed to any particular place. They bear Talman's signature of an oval vestibule or hall opening by a screen to the staircase, anticipating the 'Trianon' designs by ten years.

19. No one but Talman could have designed this doorway that originally led into the main hall of Swallowfield Park, Berkshire; a type of decorative baroque embellishment that Talman particularly favoured, as on the west terrace at Chatsworth.

20. This crude drawing is the only view of Swallowfield showing it before Atkinson encased it in cement in 1820. It was begun in 1689 for Lord Clarendon.

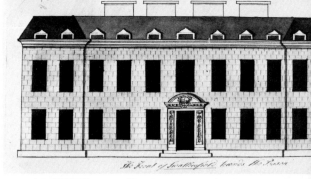

21. Swallowfield in the late eighteenth century when lived in by John Dodd. The advance and recession of the front with its layered pediments demonstrates how Talman endeavoured to make an otherwise commonplace red brick, hipped-roof house, uncommon.

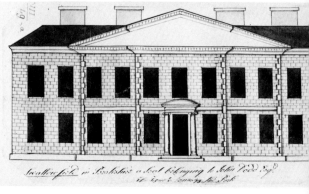

(above) The south front of Chatsworth; a grand demonstration and combination of sobriety and ~~m~~gnificence. In 1687 it was the first real baroque country house in England.

(below) The mystery about Thoresby House, Nottinghamshire, will probably never be finally ~~solv~~ed, although Talman may have played some role in its form as engraved here in *Vitruvius* ~~Bri~~*tannicus* in 1717.

The Elevation of Thoresby house in the County of Nottingham the Seat of the R.t Hon.ble the Marquiss of Dorchester to whom this plate is most humbly Inscribed

Campbell Delin.

Elevation de la Maison de Thorsby dans la Comté de Nottingham

4. (left) The west terrace at Chatsworth, laid down before Talman was dismissed in 1696. The authorship of the front above it, built from 1700, is uncertain. The stairs hint at what those at Dyrham would have looked like if built.

5. (above) The Great Stairs at Chatsworth display Talman's love of sculptural accompaniments in important rooms like halls and staircases. It was begun in 1687 and the statues of Lucrece and Apollo are by Gibbs.

26. (above) The State Drawing Room at
Chatsworth, probably the happiest fusion of the
arts of the painter, woodcarver and architect.

27. (above right) The State Dining Room at
Chatsworth with its finely carved chimney
overmantel by Samuel Watson, a carver as go
as Grinling Gibbons.

28. (lower right) The Heaven Room at Burgh
House, Northamptonshire, belonging to the s
of apartments remodelled by Talman before
1688. Antonio Verrio's illusionist painting is
baroque as his work in the chapel at Windsor
Castle.

29. These carved doors in the State Dressing Room at Burghley can be matched in style by the drawings made, but not executed, by Gibbons for state apartments at Hampton Court before 1689.

30. Dyrham Park, Gloucestershire, completed about 1700. The eclectic east

31. Orangery or greenhouse at Dyrham Park – an epitome of the Grand Trianon and relative of the chapel at Bretby, attributed to Talman.

32. Waldershare Park, Kent before the fire of 1913. Attribution to Talman is tentative, but the numerous Talmanic details tip the balance between him and John James in his favour.

33. The plainer entrance front of Waldershare Park, Kent, showing more effectively the chimney stacks linked by an arch – as at Appuldurcombe.

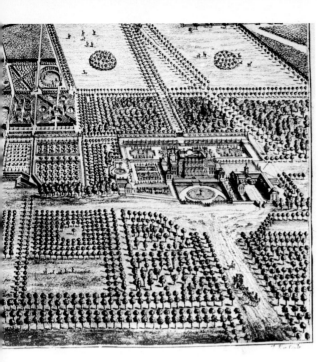

34. (left) Waldershare Park, Kent. The sophistication of the gardens, as viewed by Thomas Badeslade *c.* 1710, suggests George London's intervention.

35. (below) Appuldurcombe House, Isle of Wight; the restored shell. One of the most idiosyncratic houses of the early eighteenth century, for long tentatively attributed to John James, who may have been a carpenter here.

36, 37. (above) The first studies for Dorchester House, Surrey. Proof that Talman's front was built for Lord Portmore before 1703 and probably *c*. 1699 is in an early nineteenth-century watercolour showing the cupolas projecting above the roof-line of the earlier house.

38. (left) One of the pair of surviving gate-piers at Dorchester House, now in a housing estate near Weybric The military trophies accorc with Portmore's status as a soldier.

39. (right) Courtyard front Drayton House, Northamptonshire, dated b contract to 1708 and signec Talman, but so close in styl one of John Talman's desig for a Trianon at Hampton Court that the possibility o intervention as designer her should not be discounted.

40. (right) John Talman's
design for the Trianon at
Hampton Court. A prettily
coloured drawing, and in
quality of draughtmanship far
better than any drawing by
William.

41. (above) The drawing for
Witham Park, Somerset, made
for Colen Campbell's *Vitruvius
Britannicus* of 1717. It was
included in the manuscript and
drawings for the book but
James Gibbs's scheme appears
in the printed work.

42. (right) Talman's rough
sketches for Witham Park,
Somerset, taken from a sheet of
studies that can be dated *c.*
1702 at the latest. Dr George
Clark and Sir James Thornhill
contributed designs, and
although James Gibbs's seems
to have been the finally
accepted one, there is grave
doubt that even his was built.

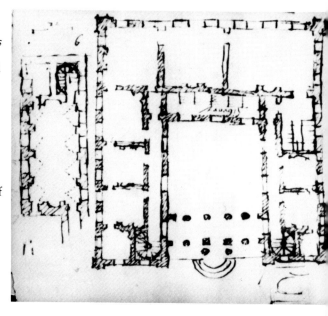

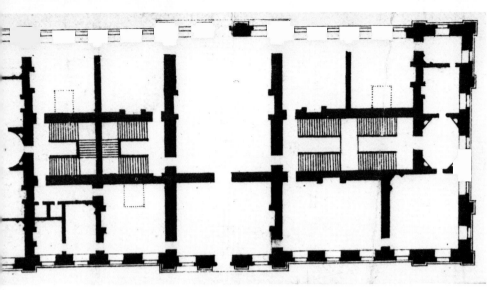

. One of the preliminary designs for Castle Howard *c*. 1699; proposing a great block-like palace
h attached porticoes and end bays framed by pilasters, and contemporary with Talman's schemes
King William at Hampton Court. The complex baroque stairs should be noted.

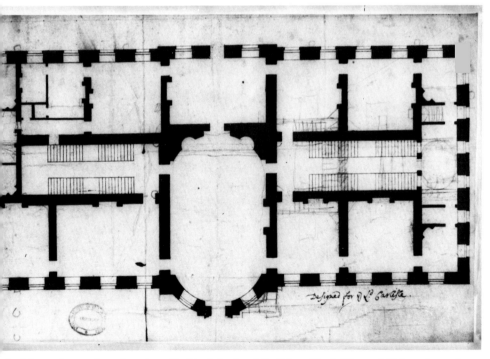

In this smaller version of a palace-like block for Lord Carlisle at Castle Howard, Talman is moving
vards greater spatiality in planning, but keeping the baroque stairs and incorporating a huge oval
oon in the Vaux le Vicomte or Château de Turny manner.

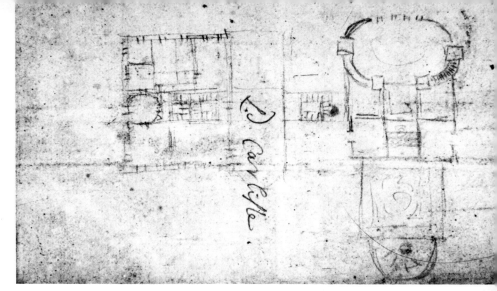

45. Rough pencil sketches for Castle Howard showing half a block-like plan next to one of a small scale, in which Talman favoured an arrangement of pavilions, an oval courtyard, secondary courts and a square main block beside a formal garden. There is just a hint here of the Villa Giulia.

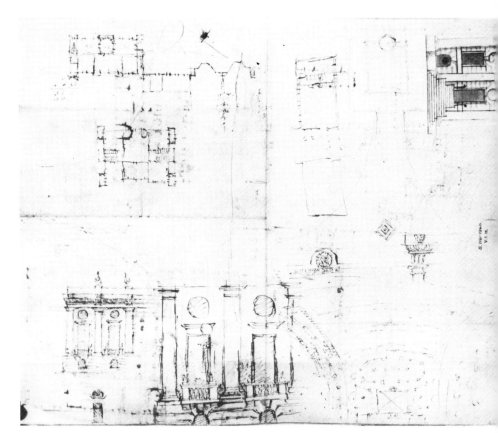

46. Many of Talman's rough studies are tantalising because they are unidentified. The plans suggest Castle Howard, therefore the three-bay pilastered pavilion could be Talman's suggestions for the square pavilions of the Villa Giulia scheme.

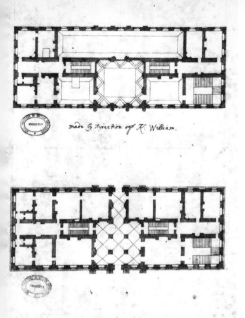

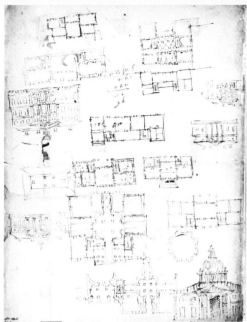

7. This is the first and most stereotyped of the
Trianon plans for King William III *c.* 1699,
probably intended to have been similar in style to
the baroque of Chatsworth. Note the stairs in the
spine of the house.

48. On this sheet are demonstrations of Talman's
fertile inventions: Palladian rotundas, proto-
Gibbsian models of houses with porticoes over
arcades, columnar episodes and porticoes *in antis*
– from a variety of engraved sources including
Palladio, Serlio and French planning.

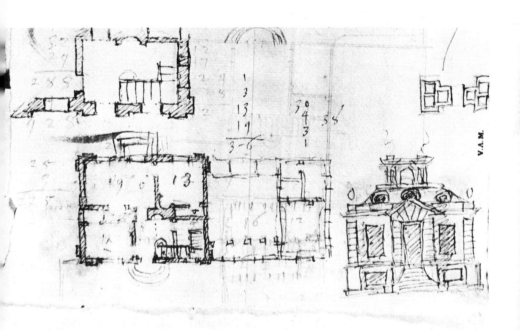

9. The first studies for George London's little house that was built on the site of the proposed Trianon.
It is still not clear if Talman built this for himself, but probably not, as none of John Talman's
correspondence is addressed to or from Thames Ditton.

50. (right) Two tantalising designs: one for a monumental front with giant columns and the other for a courtyard house of peculiarly French style, but finished off with a castellated parapet. Could this latter be for Lord Coningsby's Hampton Court, Herefordshire – a total rebuilding instead of rehabilitation?

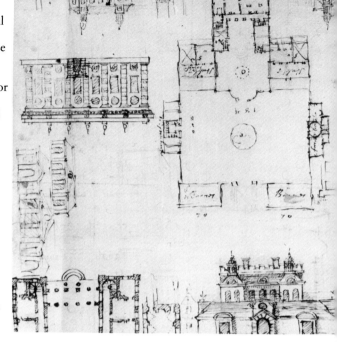

51. (below) One of the earlier idiosyncratic Trianon plans, with square pavilions at the angles linked by a niched vestibule – just as Talman had done at Hackwood as early as 1683.

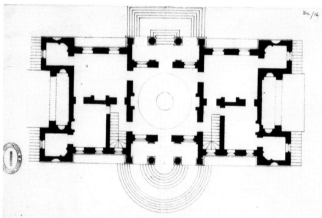

53. (above right) The plan for an alternative Trianon proje more Italianate than French plan; the staircase has a dom

54. (lower right) The domed Franco—Italianate project, showing the house sitting across a garden, identical to that proposed in the accepte Trianon scheme.

52. (right) A development of the Trianon plan with vestibules *in antis* and pavilion angles, but now with the oval niched 'tribune' in the centre. It is upon this plan that John Talman developed his project.

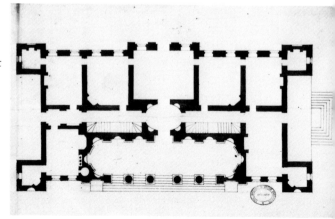

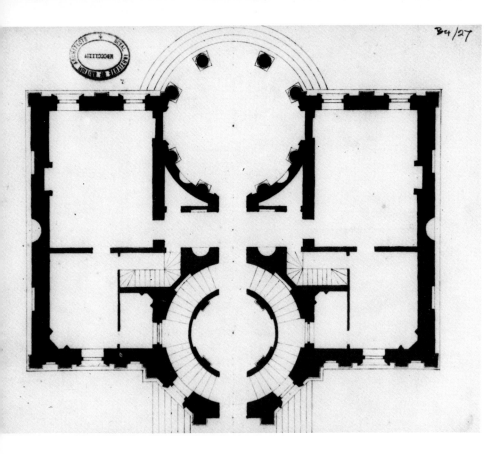

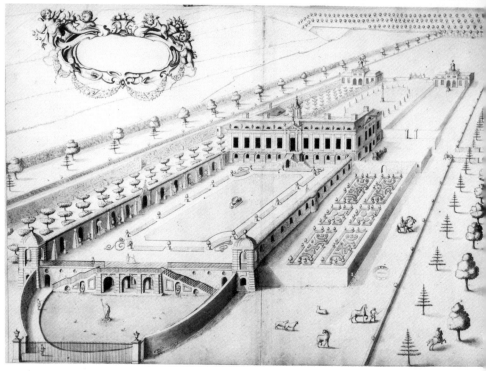

55. (above) The accepted scheme for the Trianon, in its elaborate Dutch-styled garden profusely ornamented with sculpture and topiary – a reflection, it might be said, of Talman's own collection of antique and modern sculpture.

56. (below) In this section through the Trianon the interior details are basically Dutch in inspiration and source, but drawing also upon engraved chimney-pieces by Jean Le Pautre.

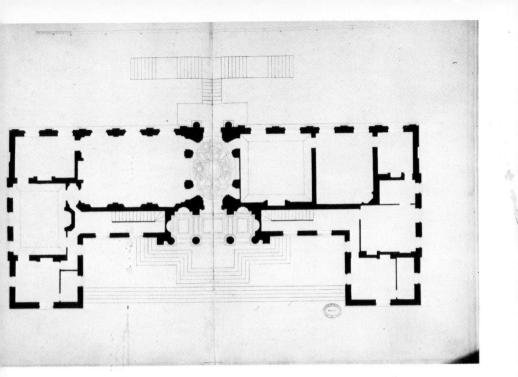

57. (above) The final plan for the Trianon; a most satisfactory demonstration of powerful spatial fluidity in the combination of oval hall and niched and shaped vestibule.

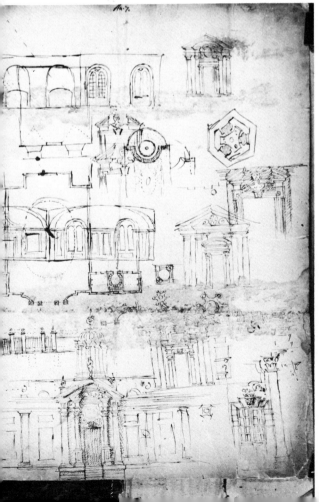

58. (left) This is one of Talman's attractive sheets of sketches, all for the accepted Trianon scheme.

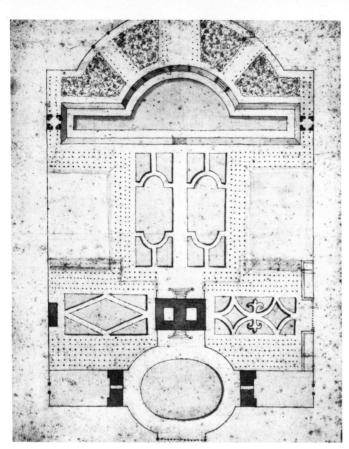

61. (above right) A more elaborate and ornamented project for the Duke of Newcastle. Once again French engravings are influential.

62. (centre right) One of the more idiosyncratic elevations for the Duke of Newcastle, this time Franco-Italianate.

63. (lower right) This plan for the Franco-Italianate project incorporates a grand baroque staircase hall of north Italian Piedmontese type.

59. The first and most stereotyped of the designs for the Duke of Newcastle. The garden is in London's style but with Talmanic episodes such as the open pavilions at the end of the canal.

60. It is not clear if this was for the Duke of Newcastle's Haughton or Welbeck, but like nearly all projects, strongly tinctured by French academic engraved sources such as Le Pautre and Marot.

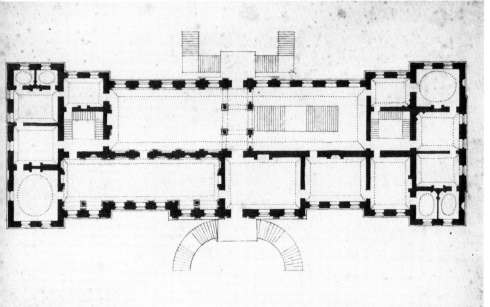

Front 207 feet

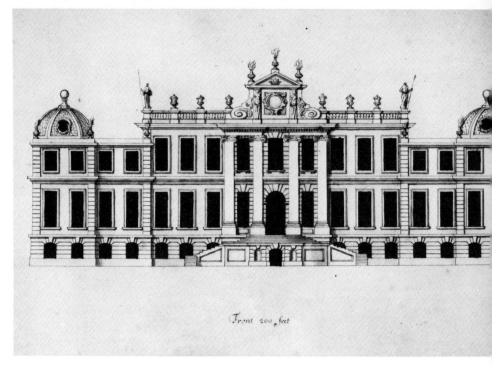

64. (above) In this Newcastle scheme Talman is perhaps at his most attractive; witness his love for sculptural and surface ornamentation. An agreeable Drayton writ large, and, of course, in 1703 Drayton was then being built.

65. (left) An e
Newcastle
elevation. The
doorway is ta
directly from
Italian sixteen
century desig
Talman's ow
collection, no
Sir John Soan
Museum.

66. The grandest and most ornamental of all the Newcastle schemes, comparable stylistically with Appuldurcombe, and a feast for the motif-mongering historian.

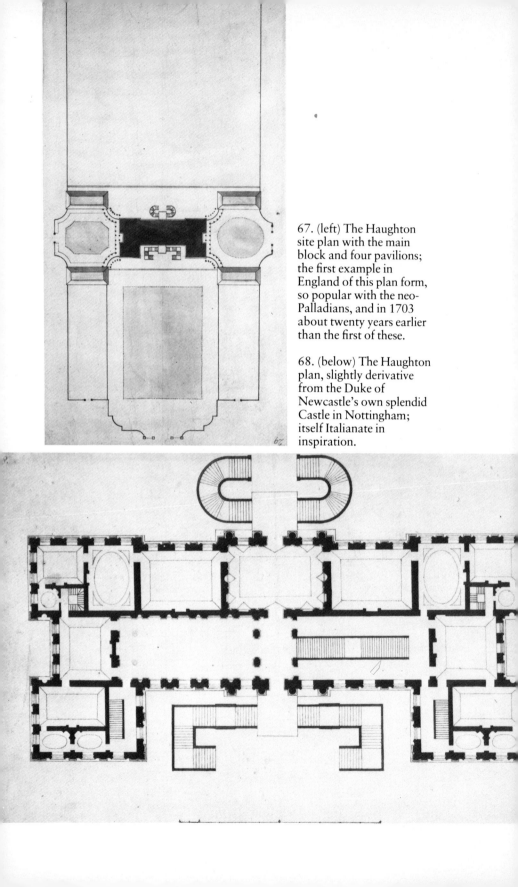

67. (left) The Haughton site plan with the main block and four pavilions; the first example in England of this plan form, so popular with the neo-Palladians, and in 1703 about twenty years earlier than the first of these.

68. (below) The Haughton plan, slightly derivative from the Duke of Newcastle's own splendid Castle in Nottingham; itself Italianate in inspiration.

69. The Haughton elevation, surely the most monumental of all Talman's palace-like schemes and in sober classical-baroque style.

70. Here is just a hint of what Haughton's Great Hall would have looked like, and can be justly compared with the type of hall being conceived in 1703 by Vanbrugh and Hawksmoor at Castle Howard.

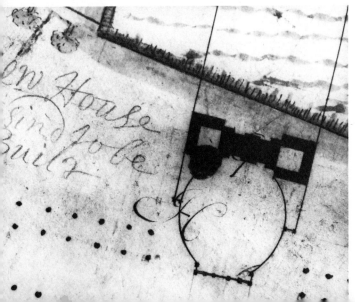

71. Upon this land survey of Kimberley Park, Norfolk, George London has scratched out his avenues, but included a vast house on a Newcastle scale.

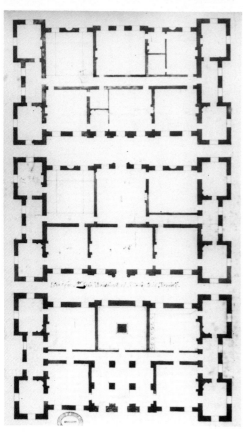

72. (left) The plans for Kimberley, as built, exce
that the four towers were probably not carried
out (unless they were rebuilt) until the middle
years of the eighteenth century.

73. (above) This detail from
photograph of Kimberley
shows the house as Talman
probably left it by *c.* 1705: a
fine example of his brick
astylism.

75. (right) Fetcham's painte
hall and staircase today, no
restored. Contemporary wi
Laguerre's painted staircase
Buckingham House, Londo

74. This is the only view of Fetcham Park, Surrey, before its
rebuilding in French renaissance style in the nineteenth century.
It was originally surrounded by a garden by George London, as
described by Celia Fiennes in her diary.

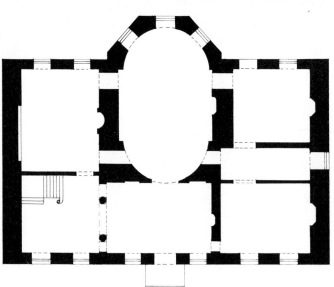

76. (above) Panton Hall, Lincolnshire, *c.* 1719, for Joseph Gace, just before its melancholy demolition. Carr added the wings to each side but the canted bay is definite by Talman.

77. (left) Jeremy Lever's restoration of what Panton looked like on plan before Carr's additions. A miniature version of the Castle Howard Château de Turny plan.

78. (above) Talman at his best in garden buildings: the bowling green temple at Chatsworth, an accompaniment to London's great parterre.

79. (left) In this detail from Kynff *c.* 1700 can be seen London's two great parterres and the bowling green with its temple. The west front is still the old Elizabethan one.

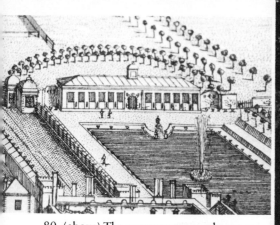

80. (above) The orangery or greenhouse at Chatsworth, begun when Talman was dismissed, but surely by him. Talman and London together enjoyed building these greenhouses.

81. (right) All that remains of the greenhouse at Castle Ashby, now in its rebuilt state beside the churchyard. Talman probably did other things at this house, so near to Drayton, before *c.* 1695, the date of the rejected contract for the north front, or after.

82. (below) These baroque stairs would probably have been built at Dyrham had William III not died and Blathwayte not found himself in financial difficulties. The garden was nevertheless an extraordinary one, by London, and full of baroque episodes.

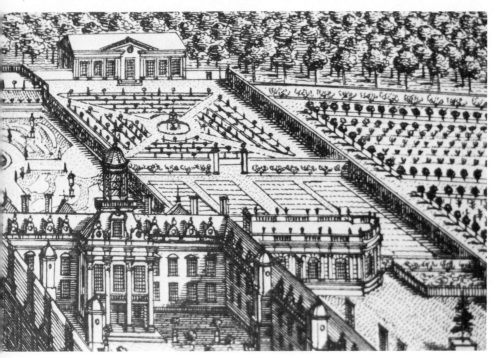

. This detail from Knyff's view of Bretby, Derbyshire, shows the chapel, certainly attributable to
Ilman, and the main cross-wing of the house whose date and authorship is disputed. It could well be
Talman as its sources are to be found in French engravings and there are other Talmanic details.

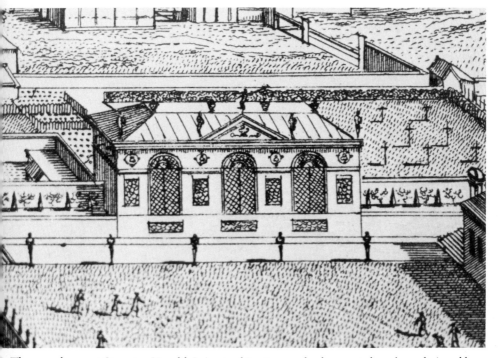

. The greenhouse at Staunton Harold, Leicestershire, in a garden known to have been designed by
eorge London.

85. The greenhouse at Dawley, Middlesex, *c.* 1700, and in a garden certainly by George London.

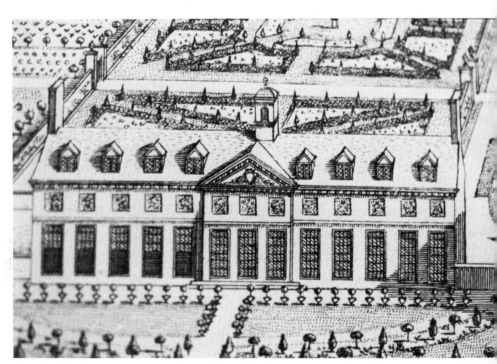

86. The greenhouse at Wimpole Hall, Cambridgeshire, again in a garden attributed to London. In a style favoured by Talman with bas-reliefs ornamenting the exterior, as at Wanstead.

7. (right) This little loggia in the gardens of Kensington Palace is almost identical to the entrance of a house in Amsterdam. It picks up the Drayton style, but so far has not been dated or its authorship confirmed.

8. (below) Barnstable, Devon. The Rolle Colonnade could hardly be by anyone else but Talman, though it is a sadly undocumented building.

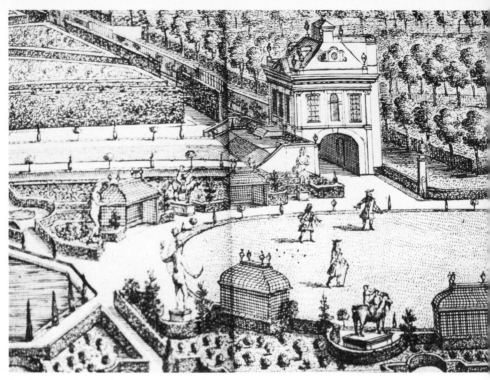

89. Wanstead's bowling green was probably the most splendid of any in England and of royal quality. It forms part of London's garden works *c.* 1707, and all the architectural accompaniments are in Talman's style. Did Jean Tijou make the ironwork?

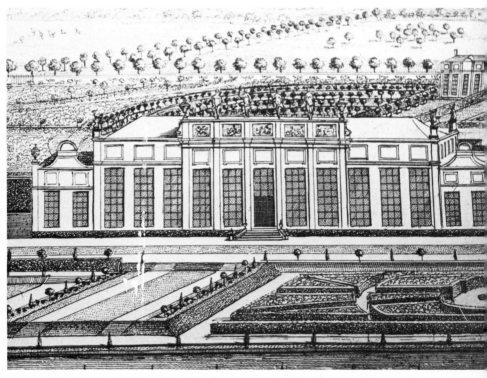

90. Talman's greenhouse at Wanstead; his finest, and admired enough by Colen Campbell to include it in his *Vitruvius Britannicus* when he was rebuilding the old mansion.